SELECTED
FROM

JAWS

PETER BENCHLEY

*Supplementary material by the staff of
Literacy Volunteers of New York City*

WRITERS' VOICES
Literacy Volunteers of New York City

WRITERS' VOICES℠ was made possible by grants from The Vincent Astor Foundation; Booth Ferris Foundation; Exxon Corporation; James Money Management, Inc.; Scripps Howard Foundation; Uris Brothers Foundation, Inc.; The H.W. Wilson Foundation; and Weil, Gotshal & Manges Foundation, Inc.

───────────**ATTENTION READERS**───────────

We would like to hear what you think about our books. Please send your comments or suggestions to:
> The Editors
> Literacy Volunteers of New York City
> 121 Avenue of the Americas
> New York, NY 10013

Selection: From JAWS by Peter Benchley. Copyright © 1974 by Peter Benchley. Used by permission of the author.

Supplementary materials © 1990 by Literacy Volunteers of New York City Inc.

Printed in the United States of America.

96 95 94 93 92 91 90 10 9 8 7 6 5 4 3 2 1

First LVNYC Printing: April 1990

ISBN 0-929631-14-5

Writers' Voices is a series of books published by Literacy Volunteers of New York City Inc., 121 Avenue of the Americas, New York, NY 10013. The words, "Writers' Voices," are a trademark of Literacy Volunteers of New York City.

Cover design by Paul Davis Studio; interior design by Barbara Huntley.
Publishing Director, LVNYC: Nancy McCord
Executive Director, LVNYC: Eli Zal

LVNYC is an affiliate of Literacy Volunteers of America.

ACKNOWLEDGMENTS

Literacy Volunteers of New York City gratefully acknowledges the generous support of the following foundations and corporations that made the publication of WRITERS' VOICES and NEW WRITERS' VOICES possible: The Vincent Astor Foundation; Booth Ferris Foundation; Exxon Corporation; James Money Management, Inc.; Scripps Howard Foundation; Uris Brothers Foundation, Inc.; The H.W. Wilson Foundation; and Weil, Gotshal & Manges Foundation Inc.

This book could not have been realized without the kind and generous cooperation of the author, Peter Benchley, and his agent, Amanda Urban, of International Creative Management, Inc.

We deeply appreciate the contributions of the following suppliers: Cam Steel Rule Die Works Inc. (steel cutting die for display); Canadian Pacific Forest Products Ltd. (text stock); Creative Graphics, Inc. (text typesetting); Horizon Paper Co., Inc. (cover stock); Martin/Friess Communications (display header); Mergenthaler Container (corrugated display); Phototype Color Graphics (cover color separations); and Ringier America Dresden Division (cover and text printing and binding).

For their guidance and assistance, we wish to thank the LVNYC Board of Directors' Publishing Committee: James E. Galton, Marvel Entertainment Group; Virginia Barber, Virginia Barber Literary Agency, Inc.; Jeff Brown; George P. Davidson, Ballantine Books; Geraldine E. Rhoads, Diamandis Communications Inc.; Virginia Rice, Reader's Digest; Martin Singerman, News America Publishing, Inc.; and Irene Yuss, Pocket Books.

Thanks also to Caron Harris and Steve Palmer of Ballantine Books for production assistance, Jeff Brown for his editorial advice and expertise, Edward Lavitt for his skill and diligence in the researching and writing of the supplementary material in this book, Margaret Ross of Universal Studios' Research Department for providing invaluable information about sharks and the making of the movie *Jaws*, and to Sergei Boissier for proofreading.

Our thanks to Paul Davis Studio and Myrna Davis, Paul Davis, and Jeanine Esposito for their inspired design of the covers of WRITERS' VOICES. Thanks also to Barbara Huntley for her sensitive attention to the interior design of this series.

And finally, special credit must be given to Marilyn Boutwell, Jean Fargo, and Gary Murphy of the LVNYC staff for their major contributions to the educational and editorial content of these books.

CONTENTS

ABOUT *WRITERS' VOICES*

"I want to read what others do—what I see people reading in libraries, on the subway, and at home."

Mamie Moore, a literacy student,
Brooklyn, New York

Writers' Voices is our response to Mamie Moore's wish:

- the wish to step forward into the reading community,
- the wish to have access to new information,
- the wish to read to her grandchildren,
- the wish to read for the joy of reading.

NOTE TO THE READER

"What we are familiar with, we cease to see. The writer shakes up the familiar scene, and, as if by magic, we see a new meaning in it."
Anaïs Nin

Writers' Voices invites you to discover new meaning. One way to discover new meaning is to learn something new. Another is to see in a new way something you already know.

Writers' Voices is a series of books. Each book contains selections from one or more writers' work. We chose the selections because the writers' voices can be clearly heard. Also, they deal with experiences that are interesting to think about and discuss.

If you are a new reader, you may want to have a selection read aloud to you, perhaps more than once. This will free you to enjoy the piece, to hear the language used, and to think about its meaning. Even if you are a more experienced reader, you may enjoy hearing the selection read aloud before reading it silently to yourself.

Each selection is set in a framework to expand your understanding of the selection. The framework includes a chapter that tells about the writer's life. Some authors write about their own lives; others write stories from their imagination. You may wonder why an author chose to write what he or she did. Sometimes you can find the answer by knowing about the author's life.

You may also find chapters about the characters, the plot, and when or where the story took place. These will help you begin thinking about the selection. They will also help you understand what may be unfamiliar to you.

We encourage you to read *actively*. An active reader does many things—while reading, and before and after reading—that help him or her better understand and enjoy a book. Here are some suggestions of things you can do:

Before Reading

• Read the front and back covers of the book, and look at the cover illustration. Ask yourself what you expect the book to be about, based on this information.

• Think about why you want to read this book. What do you want to discover, and what questions do you hope will be answered?

• Look at the contents page. Decide which chapters you want to read and in what order you want to read them.

During Reading

• Try to stay with the rhythm of the language. If you find any words or sentences you don't understand, keep reading to see if the meaning becomes clear. If it doesn't, go back and reread the difficult part or discuss it with others.

• Try to put yourself into the story.

• Ask yourself questions as you read. For example: Do I believe this story or this character? Why?

After Reading

• Ask yourself if the story makes you see any of your own experiences in a new way.

• Ask yourself if the story has given you any new information.

• Keep a journal in which you can write down your thoughts about what you have read, and save new words you have learned.

• Look over the questions at the end of the book. They are meant to help you discover more about what you have read and how it relates to you—as a person, as a reader, and as a writer. Try those questions that seem most interesting to you.

• Talk about what you have read with other readers.

Good writing should make you think after you put the book down. Whether you are a beginning reader, a more experienced reader, or a teacher of reading, we encourage you to take time to think about these books and to discuss your thoughts with others. If you want to read more books by the author of the selections, you can go to your bookstore or library to find them.

When you are finished with the book, we hope you will write to our editors about your reactions. We want to know your thoughts about our books, and what they have meant to you.

MAP OF PLACES MENTIONED
IN THE SELECTION

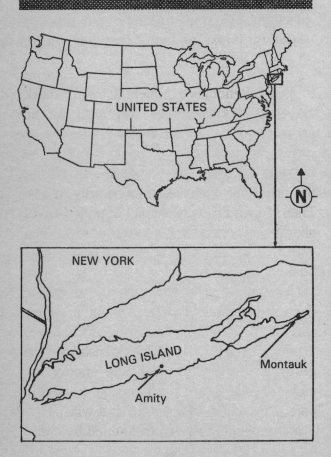

ABOUT THE SELECTION FROM
JAWS

In Peter Benchley's novel, *Jaws,* a shark attacks and kills people swimming in the ocean off Long Island, New York. This causes great fear in the community of Amity. The town sends a fisherman to kill the shark, but the fisherman vanishes mysteriously at sea. Then Martin Brody, the chief of police, takes charge. He hires Quint, a tough, shrewd man with the reputation of being the best fishing boat captain around.

Quint and Brody search for the shark for days. When they find him, Quint prepares carefully for the kill. Though Quint believes a man can always outsmart a fish, he has grown to respect this particular enemy. He and the shark are engaged in a deadly personal contest of strength and will.

Many people were so frightened by *Jaws,*

the book and the movie, that they avoided swimming in the ocean for a year or more.

Peter Benchley has had an interest in sharks for many years. He did a lot of research on shark behavior before writing this book. If you want to know more about sharks, see the chapter "About Sharks," on page 54. If you want to know more about the author, see the chapter "About Peter Benchley," on page 50. If you want to know about the movie *Jaws*, see the chapter on page 52.

Perhaps this story will remind you of a frightening experience you have had. Perhaps it will make you think about other situations where people and nature are in conflict.

SELECTED
FROM
JAWS

PETER BENCHLEY

The great fish moved silently through the night water, propelled by short sweeps of its crescent tail. The mouth was open just enough to permit a rush of water over the gills. There was little other motion: an occasional correction of the apparently aimless course by the slight raising or lowering of a pectoral fin—as a bird changes direction by dipping one wing and lifting the other. The eyes were sightless in the black, and the other senses transmitted nothing extraordinary to the small, primitive brain. The fish might have been asleep, save for the movement dictated by countless millions of years of instinctive continuity: lacking the flotation bladder common to other fish and the fluttering flaps to push oxygen-bearing water through its gills, it survived only by moving. Once stopped, it would sink to the bottom and die of anoxia.

The land seemed almost as dark as the water, for there was no moon. All that separated sea from shore was a long, straight stretch of beach—so white that it shone. From a house behind the grass-splotched dunes, lights cast yellow glimmers on the sand.

The front door to the house opened, and a man and a woman stepped out onto the wooden porch. They stood for a moment staring at the sea, embraced quickly, and scampered down the few steps onto the sand. The man was drunk, and he stumbled on the bottom step. The woman laughed and took his hand, and together they ran to the beach.

"First a swim," said the woman, "to clear your head."

"Forget my head," said the man. Giggling, he fell backward onto the sand, pulling the woman down with him. They fumbled with each other's clothing, twined limbs around limbs, and thrashed with urgent ardor on the cold sand.

Afterward, the man lay back and closed his eyes. The woman looked at him and smiled. "Now, how about that swim?" she said.

"You go ahead. I'll wait for you here."

The woman rose and walked to where the gentle surf washed over her ankles. The water was colder than the night air, for it was only mid-June. The woman called back, "You're sure you don't want to come?" But there was no answer from the sleeping man.

She backed up a few steps, then ran at the water. At first her strides were long and graceful, but then a small wave crashed into her knees. She faltered, regained her footing, and flung herself over the next waist-high wave. The water was only up to her hips, so she stood, pushed the hair out of her eyes, and continued walking until the water covered her shoulders. There she began to swim—with the jerky, head-above-water stroke of the untutored.

A hundred yards offshore, the fish sensed a change in the sea's rhythm. It did not see the woman, nor yet did it smell her. Running within the length of its body were a series of thin canals, filled with mucus and dotted with nerve endings, and these nerves detected vibrations and signaled the brain. The fish turned toward shore.

The woman continued to swim away from the beach, stopping now and then to check her position by the lights shining from the house. The tide was slack, so she had not moved up or down the beach. But she was tiring, so she rested for a moment, treading water, and then started for shore.

The vibrations were stronger now, and the fish recognized prey. The sweeps of its tail quickened, thrusting the giant body forward with a speed that agitated the tiny phosphorescent animals in the water and caused them to glow, casting a mantle of sparks over the fish.

The fish closed on the woman and hurtled

past, a dozen feet to the side and six feet below the surface. The woman felt only a wave of pressure that seemed to lift her up in the water and ease her down again. She stopped swimming and held her breath. Feeling nothing further, she resumed her lurching stroke.

The fish smelled her now, and the vibrations—erratic and sharp—signaled distress. The fish began to circle close to the surface. Its dorsal fin broke water, and its tail, thrashing back and forth, cut the glassy surface with a hiss. A series of tremors shook its body.

For the first time, the woman felt fear, though she did not know why. Adrenaline shot through her trunk and her limbs, generating a tingling heat and urging her to swim faster. She guessed that she was fifty yards from shore. She could see the line of white foam where the waves broke on the beach. She saw the lights in the house, and for a comforting moment she thought she saw someone pass by one of the windows.

The fish was about forty feet away from

the woman, off to the side, when it turned suddenly to the left, dropped entirely below the surface, and, with two quick thrusts of its tail, was upon her.

At first, the woman thought she had snagged her leg on a rock or a piece of floating wood. There was no initial pain, only one violent tug on her right leg. She reached down to touch her foot, treading water with her left leg to keep her head up, feeling in the blackness with her left hand. She could not find her foot. She reached higher on her leg, and then she was overcome by a rush of nausea and dizziness. Her groping fingers had found a nub of bone and tattered flesh. She knew that the warm, pulsing flow over her fingers in the chill water was her own blood.

Pain and panic struck together. The woman threw her head back and screamed a guttural cry of terror.

The fish had moved away. It swallowed the woman's limb without chewing. Bones and meat passed down the massive gullet in a single spasm. Now the fish turned again, homing on the stream of blood flushing from the woman's femoral artery, a beacon as clear and true as a lighthouse on a cloudless night. This time the fish attacked from below. It hurtled up under the woman, jaws agape. The great conical head struck her like a locomotive, knocking her up out of the water. The jaws snapped shut around her torso, crushing bones and flesh and organs into a jelly. The fish, with the woman's body in its mouth, smashed down on the water with a thunderous splash, spewing foam and blood and phosphorescence in a gaudy shower.

Below the surface, the fish shook its head from side to side, its serrated triangular teeth sawing through what little sinew still resisted. The corpse fell apart. The fish swallowed, then turned to continue feeding. Its brain still registered the signals of nearby prey. The water was laced with blood and shreds of flesh, and the fish could not sort signal from substance. It cut back and forth through the dissipating cloud of blood, opening and closing its mouth, seining for a random morsel. But by now, most of the pieces of the corpse had dispersed. A few sank slowly, coming to rest on the sandy bottom, where they moved lazily in the current. A few drifted away just below the surface, floating in the surge that ended in the surf.

* * *

Brody took a phone book from the top drawer of his desk and opened it to the Qs. He ran his finger down the page. "Here it is. 'Quint.' That's all it says. No first name. But it's the only one on the page. Must be him." He dialed the number.

"Quint," said a voice.

"Mr. Quint, this is Martin Brody. I'm the chief of police over in Amity. We have a problem."

"I've heard."

"The shark was around again today."

"Anybody get et?"

"Yes."

"Fish that big needs a lot of food," said Quint.

"Have you seen the fish?"

"Nope. Looked for him a couple times, but I couldn't spend too much time looking. My people don't spend their money for looking. They want action."

"How did you know how big it is?"

"I hear tell. Sort of averaged out the estimates and took off about eight feet. That's still a piece of fish you got there."

"I know. What I'm wondering is whether you can help us."

"I know. I thought you might call."

"Can you?"

"That depends."

"On what?"

"On how much you're willing to spend, for one thing."

"We'll pay whatever the going rate is. Whatever you charge by the day. We'll pay you by the day until we kill the thing."

"I don't think so," said Quint. "I think this is a premium job."

"What does that mean?"

"My everyday rate's two hundred a day. But this is special. I think you'll pay double."

"Not a chance."

"Good-by."

"Wait a minute! Come on, man. Why are you holding me up?"

"You got no place else to go."

"There are other fishermen."

Brody heard Quint laugh—a short, derisive bark. "Sure there are," said Quint. "You already sent one. Send another one. Send half a dozen more. Then when you come back to me again, maybe you'll even pay triple. I got nothing to lose by waiting."

"I'm not asking for any favors," Brody said. "I know you've got a living to make. But this fish is killing people. I want to stop it. I want to save lives. I want your help. Can't you at least treat me the way you treat regular clients?"

"You're breaking my heart," said Quint. "You got a fish needs killing, I'll try to kill it for you. No guarantees, but I'll do my best. And my best is worth four hundred dollars a day."

Brody sighed. "I don't know that the selectmen will give me the money."

"You'll find it somewhere."

"How long do you think it'll take to catch the fish?"

"A day, a week, a month. Who knows? We may never find him. He may go away."

* * *

The sea was as flat as gelatin. There was no whisper of wind to ripple the surface. The sun sucked shimmering waves of heat from the water. Now and then, a passing tern would plunge for food, and rise again, and the wavelets from its dive became circles that grew without cease.

Brody looked up at the figure on the flying bridge: Quint. He wore a white T-shirt, faded blue-jean trousers, white socks, and a pair of graying Top-Sider sneakers. Brody guessed Quint was about fifty, and though surely he had once been twenty and would one day be sixty, it was impossible to imagine what he would look like at either of those ages. His present age seemed the age he should always be, should always have been. He was about six feet four and very lean— perhaps 180 or 190 pounds. His head was totally bald—not shaven, for there were no telltale black specks on his scalp, but as bald as if he had never had any hair—and when, as now, the sun was high and hot, he wore a Marine Corps fatigue cap. His face, like the rest of him, was hard and sharp. It was ruled by a long, straight nose. When he looked down from the flying bridge, he seemed to aim his eyes—the darkest eyes Brody had ever seen—along the nose as if it were a rifle barrel. His skin was permanently browned and creased by wind and salt and sun. He gazed off the stern, rarely blinking, his eyes fixed on the slick.

A trickle of sweat running down Brody's chest made him stir. He turned his head, wincing at the sting in his neck, and tried to stare at the slick. But the reflection of the sun on the water hurt his eyes, and he turned away. "I don't see how you do it, Quint," he said. "Don't you ever wear sunglasses?"

Quint looked down and said, "Never." His tone was completely neutral, neither friendly nor unfriendly. It did not invite conversation.

But Brody was bored, and he wanted to talk. "How come?"

"No need to. I see things the way they are. That's better."

Brody looked at his watch. It was a little after two: three or four more hours before they would give up for the day and go home. "Do you have a lot of days like this?" The excitement and anticipation of the early morning had long passed, and Brody was sure they would not sight the fish that day.

"Like what?"

"Like this. When you sit all day long and nothing happens."

"Some."

"And people pay you even though they never catch a thing."

"Those are the rules."

"Even if they never get a bite?"

Quint nodded. "That doesn't happen too often. There's generally something that'll take a bait. Or something we can stick."

"Stick?"

"With an iron." Quint pointed to the harpoons on the bow.

Brody said, "What kinds of things do you stick, Quint?"

"Anything that swims by."

* * *

When he drove up to the dock, Quint was waiting for him—a tall, impassive figure whose yellow oilskins shone under the dark sky. He was sharpening a harpoon dart on a Carborundum stone.

"I almost called you," Brody said as he pulled on his slicker. "What does this weather mean?"

"Nothing," said Quint. "It'll let up after a while. Or even if it doesn't, it don't matter. He'll be there."

Brody looked up at the scudding clouds. "Gloomy enough."

"Fitting," said Quint, and he hopped aboard the boat.

"Is it just us?"

"Just us. You expecting somebody else?"

"No. But I thought you liked an extra pair of hands."

"You know this fish as well as any man, and more hands won't make no difference now. Besides, it's nobody else's business."

Brody stepped from the dock onto the

transom, and was about to jump down to the deck when he noticed a canvas tarpaulin covering something in a corner. "What's that?" he said, pointing.

"Sheep." Quint turned the ignition key. The engine coughed once, caught, and began to chug evenly.

"What for?" Brody stepped down onto the deck. "You going to sacrifice it?"

Quint barked a brief, grim laugh. "Might at that," he said. "No, it's bait. Give him a little breakfast before we have at him. Undo my stern line." He walked forward and cast off the bow and spring lines.

The water off Montauk was rough, for the wind—from the southeast now—was at odds with the tide. The boat lurched through the waves, its bow pounding down and casting a mantle of spray. The dead sheep bounced in the stern.

When they reached the open sea, heading southwest, their motion was eased. The rain had slacked to a drizzle, and with each moment there were fewer whitecaps tumbling from the top of waves.

They had been around the point only fifteen minutes when Quint pulled back on the throttle and slowed the engine.

Brody looked toward shore. In the growing light he could see the water tower clearly— a black point rising from the gray strip of land. The lighthouse beacon still shone. "We're not out as far as we usually go," he said.

"No."

"We can't be more than a couple of miles offshore."

"Just about."

"So why are you stopping?"

"I got a feeling." Quint pointed to the left, to a cluster of lights farther down the shore. "That's Amity there."

"So?"

"I don't think he'll be so far out today. I think he'll be somewhere between here and Amity."

"Why?"

"Like I said, it's a feeling. There's not always a why to these things."

"Two days in a row we found him farther out."

"Or he found us."

"I don't get it, Quint. For a man who says there's no such thing as a smart fish, you're making this one out to be a genius."

"I wouldn't go that far."

Brody bristled at Quint's sly, enigmatic tone. "What kind of game are you playing?"

"No game. If I'm wrong, I'm wrong."

"And we try somewhere else tomorrow." Brody half hoped Quint would be wrong, that there would be a day's reprieve.

"Or later today. But I don't think we'll have to wait that long." Quint cut the engine, went to the stern, and lifted a bucket of chum onto the transom. "Start chummin'," he said, handing Brody the ladle. He uncovered the sheep, tied a rope around its neck, and lay it on the gunwale. He slashed its stomach and flung the animal overboard, letting it drift twenty feet from the boat before securing the rope to an after cleat. Then he went forward, unlashed two barrels, and carried them, and their coils of ropes and harpoon darts, back to the stern. He set the barrels on each side of the transom, each next to its own rope, and slipped one dart onto the wooden throwing shaft. "Okay," he said. "Now let's see how long it takes."

The sky had lightened to full, gray daylight, and in ones and twos the lights on the shore flicked off.

The stench of the mess Brody was ladling overboard made his stomach turn, and he wished he had eaten something—anything—before he left home.

Quint sat on the flying bridge, watching the rhythms of the sea.

Brody's butt was sore from sitting on the hard transom, and his arm was growing weary from the dipping and emptying of the ladle. So he stood up, stretched, and facing off the stern, tried a new scooping motion with the ladle.

Suddenly he saw the monstrous head of the fish—not five feet away, so close he could reach over and touch it with the ladle—black eyes staring at him, silver-gray snout pointing at him, gaping jaw grinning at him. "Oh, God!" Brody said, wondering in his shock how long the fish had been there before he had stood up and turned around. "There he is!"

Quint was down the ladder and at the stern in an instant. As he jumped onto the transom, the fish's head slipped back into the water and, a second later, slammed into the transom. The jaws closed on the wood, and the head shook violently from side to side. Brody grabbed a cleat and held on, unable to look away from the eyes. The boat shuddered and jerked each time the fish moved its head. Quint slipped and fell to his knees on the transom. The fish let go and dropped beneath the surface, and the boat lay still again.

"He was waiting for us!" yelled Brody.

"I know," said Quint.

"How did he—"

"It don't matter," said Quint. "We've got him now."

"We've got *him?* Did you see what he did to the boat?"

"Give it a mighty good shake, didn't he?"

The rope holding the sheep tightened, shook for a moment, then went slack.

Quint stood and picked up the harpoon. "He's took the sheep. It'll be a minute before he comes back."

"How come he didn't take the sheep first?"

"He got no manners," Quint cackled. "Come on, you bastard. Come and get your due."

Brody saw fever in Quint's face—a heat that lit up his dark eyes, an intensity that drew his lips back from his teeth in a crooked smile, an anticipation that strummed the sinews in his neck and whitened his knuckles.

The boat shuddered again, and there was a dull, hollow thump.

"What's he doing?" said Brody.

Quint leaned over the side and shouted, "Come out from under there! Where are your guts? You'll not sink me before I get to you!"

"What do you mean, sink us?" said Brody. "What's he doing?"

"He's trying to chew a hole in the bottom of the damn boat, that's what! Look in the bilge. Come out, you Godforsaken sonofabitch!" Quint raised high his harpoon.

Brody knelt and raised the hatch cover over the engine room. He peered into the dark, oily hole. There was water in the bilges, but there always was, and he saw no new hole through which water could pour. "Looks okay to me," he said. "Thank God."

The dorsal fin and tail surfaced ten yards to the right of the stern and began to move again toward the boat. "There you come," said Quint, cooing. "There you come." He stood, legs spread, left hand on his hip, right hand extended to the sky, grasping the harpoon. When the fish was a few feet from the boat and heading straight on, Quint cast his iron.

The harpoon struck the fish in front of the dorsal fin. And then the fish hit the boat, knocking the stern sideways and sending Quint tumbling backward. His head struck the footrest of the fighting chair, and a trickle of blood ran down his neck. He jumped to his feet and cried, "I got you! I got you, you miserable shit!"

The rope attached to the iron dart snaked overboard as the fish sounded, and when it reached the end, the barrel popped off the transom, fell into the water, and vanished.

"He took it down with him!" said Brody.

"Not for long," said Quint. "He'll be back, and we'll throw another into him, and another, and another, until he quits. And then he's ours!" Quint leaned on the transom, watching the water.

Quint's confidence was contagious, and Brody now felt ebullient, gleeful, relieved. It was a kind of freedom, a freedom from the mist of death. He noticed the blood running down Quint's neck, and he said, "Your head's bleeding."

"Get another barrel," said Quint. "Bring it back here. And watch out for the coil. I want it to go over smooth as cream."

Brody ran forward, unlashed a barrel, slipped the coiled rope over his arm, and carried the gear to Quint.

"There he comes," said Quint, pointing to the left. The barrel came to the surface and bobbed in the water. Quint pulled the string attached to the wooden shaft and brought it aboard. He fixed the shaft to the new dart and raised the harpoon above his head. "He's coming up!"

The fish broke water a few yards from the boat. Like a rocket lifting off, snout, jaw, and pectoral fins rose straight from the water. Then the smoke-white belly, pelvic fin, and huge, salamilike claspers.

"I got you, you bastard!" cried Quint, and he threw a second iron, leaning his shoulder and back into the throw. The iron hit the fish in the belly, just as the great body began to fall forward. The belly smacked the water with a thunderous boom, sending a blinding fall of spray over the boat. "He's done!" said Quint as the second rope uncoiled and tumbled overboard.

The boat lurched once, and again, and there was the distant sound of crunching.

"Attack me, will you?" said Quint. He ran forward and started the engine. He pushed the throttle forward, and the boat moved away from the bobbing barrels.

"Has he done any damage?" said Brody.

"Some. We're riding a little heavy aft. He probably poked a hole in us. It's nothing to worry about. We'll pump her out."

"That's it, then," Brody said happily.

"What's what?"

"The fish is as good as dead."

"Not quite. Look."

Following the boat, keeping pace, were the two red wooden barrels. They did not bob. Dragged by the great force of the fish, each cut through the water, pushing a wave before it and leaving a wake behind.

"He's chasing us?" said Brody.

Quint nodded.

"Why? He can't still think we're food."

"No. He means to make a fight of it."

For the first time, Brody saw a frown of disquiet on Quint's face. It was not fear, nor true alarm, but rather a look of uneasy concern—as if, in a game, the rules had been changed without warning, or the stakes raised. Seeing the change in Quint's mood, Brody was afraid.

"Have you ever had a fish do this before?" he asked.

"Not like this, no. I've had 'em attack the boat, like I told you. But most times, once you get an iron in 'em, they stop fighting you and fight against that thing stickin' in 'em."

Brody looked astern. The boat was moving at moderate speed, turning this way and that in response to Quint's random turning of the wheel. Always the barrels kept up with them.

"All right," said Quint. "If it's a fight he wants, it's a fight he'll get." He throttled down to idling speed, jumped down from the flying bridge and up onto the transom. He picked up the harpoon. Excitement had returned to his face. "Okay, shit-eater!" he called. "Come and get it!"

The barrels kept coming, plowing through the water—thirty yards away, then twenty-five, then twenty. Brody saw the flat plain of gray pass along the starboard side of the boat, six feet beneath the surface. "He's here!" he cried. "Heading forward."

"Shit!" said Quint, cursing his misjudgment of the length of the ropes. He detached the harpoon dart from the shaft, snapped the twine that held the shaft to a cleat, hopped down from the transom, and ran forward. When he reached the bow, he bent down and tied the twine to a forward cleat, unlashed a barrel, and slipped its dart onto the shaft. He stood at the end of the pulpit, harpoon raised.

The fish had already passed out of range. The tails surfaced twenty feet in front of the boat. The two barrels bumped into the stern almost simultaneously. They bounced once, then rolled off the stern, one on each side, and slid down the sides of the boat.

Thirty yards in front of the boat, the fish turned. The head raised out of the water, then dipped back in. The tail, standing like a sail, began to thrash back and forth. "Here he comes!" said Quint.

Brody raced up the ladder to the flying bridge. Just as he got there, he saw Quint draw his right arm back and rise up on tiptoes.

The fish hit the bow head on, with a noise like a muffled explosion. Quint cast his iron. It struck the fish atop the head, over the right eye, and it held fast. The rope fed slowly overboard as the fish backed off.

"Perfect!" said Quint. "Got him in the head that time."

There were three barrels in the water

now, and they skated across the surface. Then they disappeared.

"God *damn!*" said Quint. "That's no normal fish that can sound with three irons in him and three barrels to hold him up."

The boat trembled, seeming to rise up, then dropped back. The barrels popped up, two on one side of the boat, one on the other. Then they submerged again. A few seconds later, they reappeared twenty yards from the boat.

"Go below," said Quint, as he readied another harpoon. "See if he done us any dirt up forward."

Brody swung down into the cabin. It was dry. He pulled back the threadbare carpet, saw a hatch, and opened it. A stream of water was flowing aft beneath the floor of the cabin. We're sinking, he told himself, and the memories of his childhood nightmares leaped into his mind. He went topside and said to Quint, "It doesn't look good. There's a lot of water under the cabin floor."

"I better go take a look. Here." Quint handed Brody the harpoon. "If he comes back while I'm below, stick this in him for good measure." He walked after and went below.

Brody stood on the pulpit, holding the harpoon, and he looked at the floating barrels. They lay practically still in the water, twitching now and then as the fish moved about below. How do you die? Brody said silently to the fish. He heard an electric motor start.

"No sweat," said Quint, walking forward. He took the harpoon from Brody. "He's banged us up, all right, but the pumps should take care of it. We'll be able to tow him in."

Brody dried his palms on the seat of his pants. "Are you really going to tow him in?"

"I am. When he dies."

"And when will that be?"

"When he's ready."

"And until then?"

"We wait."

Brody looked at his watch. It was eight-thirty.

For three hours they waited, tracking the barrels as they moved, ever more slowly, on a random path across the surface of the sea.

At first they would disappear every ten or fifteen minutes, resurfacing a few dozen yards away. Then their submergences grew rarer until, by eleven, they had not gone under for nearly an hour. By eleven-thirty the barrels were wallowing in the water.

The rain had stopped, and the wind had subsided to a comfortable breeze. The sky was an unbroken sheet of gray.

"What do you think?" said Brody. "Is he dead?"

"I doubt it. But he may be close enough to it for us to throw a rope 'round his tail and drag him till he drowns."

Quint took a coil of rope from one of the barrels in the bow. He tied one end to an after cleat. The other end he tied into a noose.

At the foot of the gin pole was an electric winch. Quint switched it on to make sure it was working, then turned it off again. He gunned the engine and moved the boat toward the barrels. He drove slowly, cautiously, prepared to veer away if the fish attacked. But the barrels lay still.

Quint idled the engine when he came

alongside the barrels. He reached overboard with a gaff, snagged a rope, and pulled a barrel aboard. He tried to untie the rope from the barrel, but the knot had been soaked and strained. So he took his knife from the sheath at his belt and cut the rope. He stabbed the knife into the gunwale, freeing his left hand to hold the rope, his right to shove the barrel to the deck.

He climbed onto the gunwale, ran the rope through a pulley at the top of the gin pole and down the pole to the winch. He took a few turns around the winch, then flipped the starter switch. As soon as the slack in the rope was taken up, the boat heeled hard to starboard, dragged down by the weight of the fish.

"Can that winch handle him?" said Brody.

"Seems to be. It'd never haul him out of the water, but I bet it'll bring him up to us." The winch was turning slowly, humming, taking a full turn every three or four seconds. The rope quivered under the strain, scattering drops of water on Quint's shirt.

Suddenly the rope started coming too fast.

It fouled on the winch, coiling in snarls. The boat snapped upright.

"Rope break?" said Brody.

"Shit no!" said Quint, and now Brody saw fear in his face. "The sonofabitch is coming up!" He dashed to the controls and threw the engine into forward. But it was too late.

The fish broke water right beside the boat, with a great rushing whoosh of noise. It rose vertically, and in an instant of horror Brody gasped at the size of the body. Towering overhead, it blocked out the light. The pectoral fins hovered like wings, stiff and straight, and as the fish fell forward, they seemed to be reaching out to Brody.

The fish landed on the stern of the boat with a shattering crash, driving the boat beneath the waves. Water poured in over the transom. In seconds, Quint and Brody were standing in water up to their hips.

The fish lay there, its jaw not three feet from Brody's chest. The body twitched, and in the black eye, as big as a baseball, Brody thought he saw his own image reflected.

"God damn your black soul!" screamed

Quint. "You sunk my boat!" A barrel floated into the cockpit, the rope writhing like a gathering of worms. Quint grabbed the harpoon dart at the end of the rope and, with his hand, plunged it into the soft white belly of the fish. Blood poured from the wound and bathed Quint's hands.

The boat was sinking. The stern was completely submerged, and the bow was rising.

The fish rolled off the stern and slid beneath the waves. The rope, attached to the dart Quint had stuck into the fish, followed.

Suddenly, Quint lost his footing and fell backward into the water. "The knife!" he cried, lifting his left leg above the surface, and Brody saw the rope coiled around Quint's foot.

Brody looked to the starboard gunwale. The knife was there, embedded in the wood. He lunged for it, wrenched it free, and turned back, struggling to run in the deepening water. He could not move fast enough. He watched in helpless terror as

Quint, reaching toward him with grasping fingers, eyes wide and pleading, was pulled slowly down into the dark water.

For a moment there was silence, except for the sucking sound of the boat slipping gradually down. The water was up to Brody's shoulders, and he clung desperately to the gin pole. A seat cushion popped to the surface next to him, and he grabbed it.

Brody saw the tail and dorsal fin break the surface twenty yards away. The tail waved once left, once right, and the dorsal fin moved closer. "Get away, damn you!" Brody yelled.

The fish kept coming, barely moving, closing in. The barrels and skeins of rope trailed behind.

The gin pole went under, and Brody let go of it. He tried to kick over to the bow of the boat, which was almost vertical now. Before he could reach it, the bow raised even higher, then quickly and soundlessly slid beneath the surface.

Brody clutched the cushion, and he found that by holding it in front of him, his forearms across it, and by kicking constantly, he could stay afloat without exhausting himself.

The fish came closer. It was only a few feet away, and Brody could see the conical snout. He screamed, an ejaculation of hopelessness, and closed his eyes, waiting for an agony he could not imagine.

Nothing happened. He opened his eyes. The fish was nearly touching him, only a foot or two away, but it had stopped. And then, as Brody watched, the steel-gray body began to recede downward into the gloom. It seemed to fall away, an apparition evanescing into darkness.

Brody put his face into the water and opened his eyes. Through the stinging salt-water mist he saw the fish sink in a slow and graceful spiral, trailing behind it the body of Quint—arms out to the sides, head thrown back, mouth open in mute protest.

The fish faded from view. But, kept from sinking into the deep by the bobbing barrels, it stopped somewhere beyond the reach of light, and Quint's body hung suspended, a shadow twirling slowly in the twilight.

Brody watched until his lungs ached for air. He raised his head, cleared his eyes, and sighted in the distance the black point of the water tower. Then he began to kick toward shore.

ABOUT
PETER BENCHLEY

Peter Benchley was born on May 8, 1940, in New York City. His father, Nathaniel, was a well-known writer, as was his grandfather, Robert. When Peter was 15, his father made him a special offer. If Peter would spend his summer vacation writing, his father would pay him. With that start, Peter Benchley went on to become a famous writer himself.

Personal experience has given him ideas for his writing. When Peter Benchley finished college, he took a trip around the world. His first book, *Time and a Ticket*, described his adventures in France, Israel, India, and other faraway places.

Benchley began his journalism career at a newspaper, where he wrote obituaries. He went on to write for *Newsweek* magazine, and later had a job in the White House writing speeches for President Lyndon B. Johnson. After that, he began to write on his own, full-time.

Benchley wanted to combine in his writing his interest in travel and adventure, and so he wrote about places he had visited. For *National Geographic* magazine, he wrote about diving for sunken ships in Bermuda.

In 1971, Peter Benchley got the idea for *Jaws*. He liked to fish, and had become interested in sharks. Then he read in a newspaper about a fisherman who had caught a 4,500-pound great white shark.

Jaws, his first novel, is about a great white shark that threatens a resort town. The novel became a best seller around the world. It was made into a very successful movie, for which Peter Benchley helped write the screenplay.

Peter Benchley writes at home in Princeton, New Jersey, where he lives with his wife and three children.

ABOUT THE MOVIE
JAWS

The moviemakers wanted the film of *Jaws* to be as exciting and realistic as possible. To do this, they had to do things that had never been done before.

In the past, many movies that took place at sea were actually filmed in studios. Small models of ships were put in large tanks of water and filmed there. Sometimes these models looked real when the film was shown. But often they didn't.

For *Jaws*, the moviemakers decided to use real boats and real sharks in the ocean. But the sharks became their first big problem. Some fish, like dolphins, can be trained to perform. But real sharks can't be trained. The moviemakers finally decided to make artificial sharks that would look real.

These sharks were made of steel, shaped and painted to look like sharks. They were 25 feet long, weighed 2,000 pounds, and contained wires, tubes, and motors. They could be made to dive, bite, chew, turn their heads, flip their tails, and behave like real sharks. At first, of course, there were problems getting things to work right. But engineers adjusted the delicate controls. In time the operators were able to make the fake sharks do everything the script required.

Scientists who study sharks were asked to look at scenes from the movie. These experts said they could not tell the fake sharks from real ones.

The moviemakers had many other problems. They had to deal with bad weather and stormy seas. There were many days when they could not film at all. But *Jaws* eventually became the hit film everyone had hoped for, thrilling and frightening audiences because it seemed so real.

ABOUT
SHARKS

The triangular fin cutting through the water, the enormous gaping mouth ready to bite huge chunks of fishing boats and to devour people in pieces: Are all sharks like this?

The answer is definitely *no*.

Sharks are a special kind of sea creature. While they are properly called fish, they are different from other animals that live in the waters of the world. True fish, such as tuna, salmon, and trout, have bones as a frame for their bodies. Sharks do not have bones. Their bodies are held together and supported by cartilage, a strong, flexible material.

Another difference between true fish and sharks has to do with the way they "breathe." If you have ever watched goldfish in a tank, you have probably noticed that they often remain in one place. They do not move their bodies, but continually open and close their mouths. It is as if they were gulping the water. This is how they breathe. As the water passes through their gills, the gills take in oxygen from the water. It is like the process of breathing for people, except that we get our oxygen from the air that passes through our lungs.

Most sharks, however, cannot remain still in the water and breathe. Because of the way their breathing system works, they must keep moving forward. This motion makes the water move past the sharks' gills so their bodies take up the oxygen they need to survive.

Another interesting thing about sharks is the way they locate food. Although they have eyes, they depend mostly on their senses of smell and hearing to detect the presence of food.

A shark's sense of smell is extremely keen. Scientists have said that a shark can smell one drop of blood in one million drops of water. But until there is something to smell, such as a bleeding fish or a piece of fisherman's bait, the shark will use its unusual hearing system to locate its prey.

The shark's hearing apparatus, which works somewhat like ours, is located in its head. But the shark also has very sensitive organs all along its skin. Boats, people moving on the water, fish swimming below the surface, all create low-frequency sounds that reach these sensitive organs. These sounds signal the shark's brain that something is nearby. The signals also act as a kind of homing device. They tell the shark in which direction to swim to investigate the signal that might mean his dinner.

There are more than 250 different kinds of sharks. They vary considerably in size, shape, and the food they eat.

The largest shark known, the Whale Shark, averages 35 feet in length and weighs as much as 10 tons. This is about the weight of a fully loaded truck. This enormous fish, strangely enough, has a diet that consists almost entirely of plankton, tiny plants and animals that float in water all over the world. Whale Sharks have sieve-like strainers in their mouths to catch the plankton as the sharks swim through the water.

A few specimens of a very small shark have been caught in the Pacific Ocean. These rare sharks are only four or five inches long, about the size of sardines, when fully grown.

Fishermen and scientists who study the habits of sharks have observed a pattern that sometimes takes place after a shark has spotted something to eat. The lone shark is quickly joined by others. As soon as feeding begins, when blood from the prey stains the water, they all become wild. They thrash, twist, turn, and shake their heads in a violent feeding frenzy. Sharks have been observed eating each other in these wild orgies.

The Great White Shark is thought of as the classic man-eater. It can grow to be more than 20 feet long, and may weigh more than three tons. Swimmers have been attacked by Great Whites all over the world— from New Jersey to California to Australia.

But Great Whites are not really hunting people. Some attacks are cases of mistaken identity. The shark thinks the swimmer is a sea lion. Others are accidents: The shark just wants to taste this strange creature to see what it is.

Great Whites now have such a bad reputation that they have been hunted and killed almost to the point of extinction.

This information about sharks need not be frightening. After all, millions of people fish, swim, and go boating in the oceans of the world. Rarely do any of them ever *see* a shark, much less get attacked by one. And, of course, most species of shark are not people eaters!

The best advice about sharks comes from Jacques-Yves Cousteau, the world-renowned expert on deep sea diving. He has had many close encounters with sea creatures of all sorts. "Sharks are unpredictable," Cousteau says. "If you enter a shark's domain: be careful!"

GLOSSARY

Bow. The front end of a boat.

Chum. Cut-up bait.

Flying bridge. An open platform on top of a boat's pilothouse.

Gaff. A hook with a handle used to help land large fish.

Gin pole. A support for raising or moving heavy weights.

Gunwale. The top edge of a boat's side.

Starboard. The right-hand side of a boat. The left-hand side is port.

Stern. The rear end of a boat.

Transom. The flat framework across the stern of a boat.

QUESTIONS FOR THE READER

Thinking about the Story

1. What did you think about the selection from *Jaws*? What did you like or not like?

2. Are there ways that the events or people in the selection became important or special to you? Write about or discuss these.

3. In what ways did the selection answer the questions you had before you began reading

4. Were any parts of the selection from *Jaws* difficult to understand? If so, you may want to read or listen to them again. You might think about why they were difficult.

Thinking about the Writing

1. How did Peter Benchley help you see, hear, and feel what happened in the selection? Find

the words, phrases, or sentences that did this best.

2. Writers think carefully about their stories' characters and events. In writing this selection, what do you think Peter Benchley felt was most important? Find the parts of the story that support your opinion.

3. Which character in the selection was most interesting to you? How did Peter Benchley help you learn about this person? Find the places in the selection where you learned the most about this person.

4. In the selection, Peter Benchley uses dialogue. Dialogue can make a story stronger and more alive. Pick out some dialogue that you feel is strong, and explain how it helps the story.

5. In *Jaws*, Peter Benchley creates a feeling of terror. Right from the beginning, you have a feeling something terrible is about to happen. Go back to the story and find the parts that make you feel this terror.

Activities

1. Were there any words that were difficult for you in the selection from *Jaws*? Go back and try

to figure out their meanings. Discuss what you think each word means, and why you made that guess. Discuss with your teacher or another student how you are going to remember each word. Some ways to remember words are to put them on file cards, or write them in your journal, or create a personal dictionary. Be sure to use the words in your writing in a way that will help you to remember their meaning.

2. How did you help yourself understand the selection? Did you ask yourself questions? What were they? Discuss these questions with other people who have read the same selection, or write about them in your journal.

3. Talking with other people about what you have read can increase your understanding of it. Discussion can help you organize your thoughts, get new ideas, and rethink your original ideas. Discuss your thoughts about the selection with someone else who has read it. Find out if your opinions are the same or different. See if your thoughts change as a result of this discussion.

4. After you finish reading or listening, you might want to write down your thoughts about the book. You could write a book review, or a

letter to a friend you think might be interested in *Jaws*. You could write your reflections on the book in your journal, or you could write about topics the book has brought up that you want to explore further.

5. Did reading the selection give you any ideas for your own writing? You might want to write about:

• a frightening experience you actually had.

• a conflict between people and nature that you have observed.

• something you imagine would scare another reader.

6. You might want to put together a presentation on other dangerous animals, such as snakes, or lions, or bears. You could read books about these animals, or go to a natural history museum or zoo to learn about them. You might cut pictures out of magazines to illustrate your report.

WRITERS' VOICES

Kareem Abdul-Jabbar and Peter Knobler, *Selected from GIANT STEPS*, $3.50

Rudolfo A. Anaya, *Selected from BLESS ME, ULTIMA*, $3.50

Maya Angelou, *Selected from I KNOW WHY THE CAGED BIRD SINGS and THE HEART OF A WOMAN*, $3.50

Peter Benchley, *Selected from JAWS*, $3.50

Carol Burnett, *Selected from ONE MORE TIME*, $3.50

Mary Higgins Clark, *Selected from THE LOST ANGEL*, $3.50

Avery Corman, *Selected from KRAMER VS. KRAMER*, $3.50

Bill Cosby, *Selected from FATHERHOOD and TIME FLIES*, $3.50

Louise Erdrich, *Selected from LOVE MEDICINE*, $3.50

Maxine Hong Kingston, *Selected from CHINA MEN and THE WOMAN WARRIOR*, $3.50

Loretta Lynn with George Vecsey, *Selected from COAL MINER'S DAUGHTER*, $3.50

Selected from CONTEMPORARY AMERICAN PLAYS, $3.50

To order, please send your check to Publishing Program, Literacy Volunteers of New York City, 121 Avenue of the Americas, New York, NY 10013. Please add $1.50 per order and .50 per book to cover postage and handling. NY and NJ residents, add appropriate sales tax. Prices subject to change without notice.